Sorrento & Pompeii Travel Guide

Attractions, Eating, Drinking, Shopping & Places To Stay

Ryan Wilson

Copyright © 2014, Astute Press
All Rights Reserved.

No part of this publication may be reproduced, stored in a retrieval system, or transmitted, in any form or by any means without the prior written permission of the publisher, nor be otherwise circulated in any form of binding or cover other than that in which it is published and without similar condition being imposed on the subsequent purchaser.

If there are any errors or omissions in copyright acknowledgements the publisher will be pleased to insert the appropriate acknowledgement in any subsequent printing of this publication.

Although we have taken all reasonable care in researching this book we make no warranty about the accuracy or completeness of its content and disclaim all liability arising from its use

Table of Contents

Sorrento 6
   Culture 8
   Location & Orientation 9
   Climate & When to Visit 10

Sightseeing Highlights 11
   Correale di Terranova Museum 11
   Piazza Tasso 12
   Cathedral of San Filippo & Giacomo 14
   Small Marina/Large Marina 15
   Baths of Regina Giovanna 16
   Via del Capo (Panoramic View) 18
   Amalfi Coast Day Trip 19
   Pompeii Historical Site 20
   Capri Island 22
   Naples 25

Recommendations for the Budget Traveller 28
   Places to Stay 28
      Sorrento 28
      Ravello (Amalfi Coast) 29
      Pompeii 30
      Naples 30
   Places to Eat 31
      Sant'anna da Emilia 31
      Zi'Antonio 32
      Taverna Azzura 32
      Gelateria Davide 33
   Places to Shop 33
      Macramé 34
      Limonoro 34
      De Cenzo 35

Pompeii 36
   Culture 37
   Location & Orientation 39
   Climate & When to Visit 39

Sightseeing Highlights...41
Ancient Ruins of Pompeii 41
Temple of Apollo 43
Temple of Jupiter 43
Temple of Isis 44
Street of Tombs..44
Stabian Baths..45
House of Menander 45
House of Lovers 46
Lupanare (Ancient Brothel) 46
Garden of Fugitives..47
Mount Vesuvius 47
Sanctuary of Madonna of the Rosary............................49
Naples Day Trip 50
Piazza del Plebiscito 51
Museo Archeologico Nazionale.................................51
Amalfi 52
Positano..53
Ravello 54
Solerno..55
Blue Grotto, Capri 56

Recommendations for the Budget Traveller 58
Places To Stay...58
Hotel Diana Pompeii 58
Hotel Forum 59
Hotel Palma 60
Albergo Pace Pompeii Hotel......................................61
Hotel Astoria 61
Places To Eat...62
Ristorante Pizzeria Carlo Alberto 62
Ristorante Al Gamberone 62

Sorrento

The lovely holiday town of Sorrento has beautiful architecture and a scenic main square with quaint cafes, restaurants and shops. On the Circumvesuviana rail line it can be easily reached from Naples. It is also an ideal base for visiting Pompeii, Herculaneum and the island of Capri.

Walk to the top of the hills of Sorrento and look across the beautiful Bay of Naples. Squint your eyes, and look for Mount Vesuvius, one of the most famous and powerful volcanoes in history.

He's quiet, for now, but every now and then a rumble, or a cloud of steam rising from the peak, to remind those who live in his shadow that he's still there. To remind yourself of the power of this massive living mountain, take a trip to Pompeii, (just a short train ride from Sorrento) and see the results of the powerful eruption that buried the town and its people for millennia.

But for now, climb back down that hill, into the sun-warmed streets of Sorrento, into the pinks and blues and coral and green, and bask in the Mediterranean food and culture that has made Sorrento a much-loved tourist city.

The oldest ruins in Sorrento date back to over three millennia ago. It was an important town for the Romans, as gorges that run a ring around the city made it easily defendable, then even after the fall of the Roman Empire, it switched sides to be placed under the control of the Byzantines, then back to Napoli, then finally to the new Italian Kingdom in 1861. Now, Sorrento is an extremely popular tourist destination that was a favorite of both Goethe and Keats.

Here you will find colorful discotheques throbbing late into the night, balanced with the sleepy afternoons of a siesta culture. Here you will find the delicious liquor limoncello, made fresh here for centuries. Here you will find shopping, and wine, and swimming in some of the most beautiful waters known to man.

Sorrento is an area of the world that has been occupied for almost as long as humans have walked upright. Go find out why.

Culture

Italia, Italia, there's no culture quite like there is there. Everything is said with a mixture of beautifully articulated speech and gestures, hands to the side, palms up with a question, shoulders shrugged way up to say "I don't know." What you do know in Italy, however, is that you will be fed, you will be taken care of, you will be given heaps and heaps of seconds and thirds, and all your senses will be satiated, smells, sounds, sights, until you close your eyes for the evening and open them again the next day to church bells ringing, and Vespas buzzing along the street.

Buon giorno says "good morning", and a smile says it all. Sorrento has been a haven for tourists and sailors for millennia, so it is safe to say that the residents here are used to wide-eyed visitors, and stuttering attempts at the local language. Even if buon giorno is all you can muster, that should be enough, and you'll find the local population helpful and generous.

Sorrento is in the south of Italy, which is remarkably different than its northern counterpoint. There are some theorists that say that Italy was never truly unified, that the North and the South remain as different as ever they were. Don't expect the hustle and bustle of the more commercial Milan, or the towering cultural monuments of Rome and Florence. Sorrento prides itself in being a coastal gem, a sometimes-quiet, sometimes-rowdy southern sister of the Italian cities, and caters to tourists from all over the world.

Expect local pizza and pastas, and fresh fish and local wines. Also expect restaurants who tailor to the hoards of visitors who descend upon Sorrento each year – wiener schnitzel to the German tourists, and noodles for the Japanese. Don't expect to have this city to yourself; its secret was leaked too long ago to fathom, but do your homework before you go to ensure that your time in Sorrento and the surrounding countryside is everything you wanted from your Italian holiday.

Location & Orientation

Sorrento is located in the south of Italy, a short train ride from Pompeii or Naples. It also has access to several of the smaller islands off the coast of Italy, such as Capri, and you can find that it's easy to reach Sorrento by car, bus, train, or boat. If you are flying, you want to take a flight to Naples Capodichino Airport, then take either a car, bus, or train from Naples to Sorrento.

You may find the train to be the most accessible, as this is what most Italians use to visit the area. You want to take the Circumvesuviana (around Vesuvius) train, which departs most days every 30 minutes and will take you about 2 hours to arrive. The cost will be about 4 Euros, so you will have plenty of money left over for a glass of wine as your train winds its way to the coast.

Climate & When to Visit

Sorrento is on the Mediterranean coast, and has a temperate climate. That said, it gets quite hot in the summer months, in July and August, which also seems to be when the majority of Northern European visitors descend upon this coastal town.

Before you visit, think about what you'd like to do when you get here. If your idea of a perfect Italian vacation is beaches, late-night discos, crowded streets, and restaurants that are open for business until the small hours of the night, you'd probably like to visit from April – August, when most of the visitors are in Sorrento, and most companies and businesses catering to the tourism trade are open and fully operational.

If you'd like a calmer, perhaps a bit chillier sojourn in Sorrento, feel free to come in the winter months. You'll be just fine with a light jacket and long trousers, and you'll have a lot of restaurants to yourself, but just be prepared for transportation options to be reduced somewhat, and some stores closed. Sorrento has a marvelous tourism website that you should check before you're thinking about visiting: http://www.sorrentotourism.com/en/index.php.

When calling the numbers below, keep in mind that the country code for Italy is +39.

Sightseeing Highlights

Correale di Terranova Museum

The 1700's was a century of pleasure and enjoyment for those who could afford it. Wigs were powdered, corsets tied tight, paintings small and intricate, necessitating a long gaze to appreciate their beauty. Take a dive into this century in this museum, which contains dozens of beautiful examples of paintings, miniatures, and porcelains to be appreciated over a long, lazy morning during your visit to Sorrento.

A wonderful place to start in your exploration of Sorrento has to be this museum, built in the 1700's on land given to the Correale family from the Queen of Aragon in 1498. It is special for so many reasons, but particularly for the collection of Neapolitan art and also the vista its land offers. From the land, you can look over and have a beautiful view of the panoramic Sorrento coast. For a first look, this is one not to miss.

The museum holds some odd hours, so it is a good idea to check the website below before you visit. Normally, it is open Wednesday through Monday from 9:30 am to 1:30, April through September. On Wednesdays and Saturdays the museum has extended hours, which may be that perfect chance to enjoy a rich, beautiful sunset from the view from the esplanade at the museum.

Address: Via Correale 50, Sorrento, 80067
Telephone 081 8781846
www.museocorreale.it

Piazza Tasso

Everyone can tell you that the piazza is the place to be, when the sun is set, and bellies are full from a delightful Italian meal, when the guitar players dust off their picks, and young artists paint their faces gold or silver or white, feigning to be statues that move when you drop a coin in their hat. It's a place to see and be seen, to listen and to sing if the spirit moves you. This is Italy, after all. Music is the mortar between the stones in every building, and with wine this cheap, you'll find yourself singing along to just about anything.

Piazza Tasso is the largest and main square of Sorrento. Inside the piazza, you can find the Cathedral of Carmine, which is open to visitors if you need a quick moment of solitude after the hustle and bustle of the piazza.

During the day, this piazza is busy with traffic, both car and pedestrian, but in the evening the piazza takes on a life of its own as police limit the amount of traffic coming through the piazza. You'll find residents here relaxing after a day of work, and enjoy a cup of coffee or glass of vino (wine) as you people-watch yourself to nirvana.

Once you've had your fill of people watching and imbibing, take a walk down Via San Cesareo, which is a busy shopping street, and carries a huge assortment of the lemon liquors and sweets that Sorrento is known for. Here you will have to try some limoncello, a liquor made of lemon zest and peel. It is sweet and sharp, and is a perfect digestive for any night on your sojourn.

Address: Corso Italia, Sorrento

Cathedral of San Filippo & Giacomo

Take a walk through the small twists and turns of the ancient city of Sorrento, and you're bound to wind up at the Duomo, or main cathedral, of the city. It is strange to think that this relatively small and understated structure is the city's most prominent religious meeting places, and has been for centuries now. But step inside, into the dim and humid interior, and you can still hear the echo of the choirs that have sung there, the tears of widows and smiles of brides, and bells ringing to harken the faithful to prayer.

You can find the Duomo on the Corso Italia, and at first its simple yet bright façade may confuse you, and you will check your map to make sure you've actually arrived at the right location. The first thing you will see is its beautiful façade; it is a surprisingly cheery yellow color, with columns as cross-sections and various sculptures dotting each side, a mark of the architecture of Borromini, a well-known architect of the time. It is unmistakably from the renaissance, and is a must on your visit to Sorrento. But step inside, and immediately the opulence you find will take you aback. You can find frescoes painted on the walls by local artists from Naples, and also a carved rendition of the Crucifixion underneath a sumptuous arch.

In the beautiful and sun-speckled interior, you can find that all surfaces, from the walls, to the floor, to the soaring ceiling above, are covered in color, inlaid wood and stone, and glass in every color imaginable. Smell the incense used during Sunday mass, used for centuries now, and creates a thick, sweet interior even on days it is not used.

The choir lofts were rebuilt in the last few centuries, and show remarkable craftsmanship and integration into the original building.

If you are there to visit, or take place in the masses that are still held in this 15th century treasure, make sure you take a shawl or cardigan, as bare shoulders are frowned upon in this sacred space.

Adddress: Largo Arcivescovado: At the corner of Corso Italia and Via. R.R. Giuliani, Sorrento

Ask at your hotel for visiting hours and time of mass.

Small Marina/Large Marina

No trip to the south of Italy, particularly in the sticky summer months, is complete without a trip to the beach. Don't expect sprawling white sparkling sand here – these beaches are located right in the city itself, and function as marinas as well as a gathering place for sun-worshippers and children splashing in and out of the water.

Because of the topography of the coastline around Sorrento, finding a beach without having to scale a cliff can be a difficult thing to do. Lucky for us Sorrento have Marina Piccola (Small Marina) and Marina Grande (Big Marina) right smack in the middle of town with beautiful beaches to visit.

Marina Piccola can be found from following Via Marina Piccola straight from Piazza Tasso, which makes it incredibly convenient. You can also find boats here that will take you on coastal excursions.

Marina Grande can be found extremely close to the Piazza della Vittoria, and is, as you can tell from the name, the larger of the two options. In fact, Marina Grande actually looks and feels like a small fishing village, and you can easily spend all day between lounging on the beach, renting a jet ski or motorboat, then wandering to the sea-facing street, choosing between the pastel-colored buildings for a bite to eat. There is no car traffic in this area, and you can drift a few centuries in the past easily during a long quiet day here.

It is an easy walk out to either Marina Piccola or Marina Grande, just ask the information desk at your hotel or hostel for directions. Wear your walking shoes; it can be a steep descent down to the Marinas, and a steep walk back, but not long at all, as the city of Sorrento is so compact.

Baths of Regina Giovanna

After a few days' basking in the noises and salty air of Sorrento, you may want to strap on some walking shoes and take a look around the gorgeous countryside around you. Sorrento is an excellent starting point for excursions both on land and by foot, and it's safe to say that boredom just isn't an option during this trip.

Legend has it that in the early 14th century, Regina Giovanna, the Queen of Naples, would come here to bathe, far away from peeping Toms. Legend further has it that she would do much more here than just bathe, history having painted her a somewhat lustful color, but one look at the baths she would visit will still even the most torrid of stories, and you can relax in the crisp, cool water in which history is so deeply soaked.

The baths are an easy trip. You take a bus to the city bus terminus, and take a small path that begins there, at the Cape of Sorrento. You can feel free to follow other tourists, or locals that look out to take a walk, as this is a popular spot for relaxation. Take a small walk, and then a climb down a steep staircase, and you will reach a beautiful lagoon, filled with clear blue water, and illuminated by the sun above. Feel free to take a dip, and wade under the natural arch that soars above the hidden lagoon. This is indeed a magical place, and floating in the cool waters, you can imagine what stories were made here, this place so conducive to secrecy and love.

There is also the ruins of a magnificent Roman villa here, built during the first century, that you can explore freely, and a larger, somewhat rocky beach that you can stretch out on after your trip to the baths.

To get here, take the bus to the Cape of Sorrento, or take the SITA bus to Massalubrense.

Via del Capo (Panoramic View)

A trip to Sorrento is certainly not complete without taking in – breathlessly – the magnificent vistas from the Via del Capo. This is best to do on a cool afternoon, when the sun is lower and the heat of the day has relatively passed you by. Step onto the Corso Italia, and go west until you can see that the street changes its name to Via del Capo. You will find yourself travelling away from the center of town, away from the hustle and bustle of traffic and car horns.

Here you will pass by some of the more expensive hotels, and also some tiny beaches. Take a pause and dip your feet in the cool water. This will rejuvenate you for the rest of your walk.

If you want to pause for dinner, stop at Marina Puolo, with its restaurants, cafés, and small, creaking fishing boats. Pass by an ancient Roman villa, now ruined, using a just as ancient rocky path.

Along your walk, look around you, out over the Bay of Naples. Look at the boats coming in from a long day of fishing, and the Bay changing color with the falling sun. You can also look back and see the view towards the Cape (Capo), and those gorgeous white limestone cliffs that will also change color and morph with the passing of the day.

Stop in a small restaurant on your way back, or sit on a beach and watch the sun set. Walking up the Via del Capo is a perfect way to end a perfect day in Italy.

Amalfi Coast Day Trip

Taking a day trip along the Amalfi Coast is an exercise in faith. You may find yourself holding your breath as the driver whips back and forth at the edge of the cliffs that extend out of Sorrento. Breathe in, hold in your breath, and let it out slowly. The driver is in control, and you are in for a journey like no other as the trip takes you up and out of Sorrento, and along some of the most beautiful strips of land known to man. It's no wonder they say mermaids used to occupy these waters, and princes and kings and adventurers alike would attempt to land on these opulent shores.

You will find that the driver or company you choose for your day tour is very flexible: if you are more interested in sampling local Italian fare, then you will find a good part of your day is spent in the local markets or even a hidden restaurant hanging off a cliff high over the valley. If you are more interested in history, you will find your driver or guide pays special attention to show you the important historical sites of the regions you visit. Make sure you talk this over when booking, as arrangements might have to be made if you find yourself straying from the usual path. Your hotel can help you book a tour, or you can speak to the company below, who has received high recommendations (including from the writer of this guide).

Make a stop in Ravello, a town as beautiful as its name suggests, which is the highest town you will find on the coast. Bring your camera – you will want to take pictures of the beautiful scenery you see from here. You will also pass by Amalfi, the namesake city of the region, whose beaches and waterfront are the stuff of paintings and songs. You might also want to take a pause in Positano, the town that was so popular with writers and artists in the middle of the last century. Take a stroll around, and take a look at the beautifully colored buildings and houses in this quiet, sleepy town. If you book with your tour company ahead of time, you might even want to stop for lunch in this idyllic town.

Check out this company, and write them about deals they might have when you're visiting.
http://www.benvenutolimos.com/

Pompeii Historical Site

There are no words to describe what it feels like to walk through a city like Pompeii. Despite the empty brothels, houses, temples, and plasters of humans, caught at the moment of their demise, there is something, a feeling in this city that is absolutely impossible to describe. It still lives, empty, hollow, yet filled with shadows of the people that once called this once bustling seaside town home. Pompeii might be one of the most powerful historical sites you will visit on your trip.

You can easily take the train, if you do not want to go with a private tour, to Pompeii. It's a 30-40 minute journey from Sorrento (disembark at Pompeii Scavi.) Once you get off the train, you will find the entrance to Pompeii a few minutes up the road, past souvenir trucks and snack stands. You may want to buy a bottle of water there. It will be fairly pricey, but there will be nothing once you get inside the actual ruins. It costs 11 Euros for a full-day pass.

The history of Pompeii is tragic. In around 200 BC, the Romans took over Pompeii, and the town was under Roman rule until its demise on August 24th, 79. When Vesuvius erupted, Pompeii was a bustling town, with markets, shops, and more than its share of brothels to attract the sailors to the city. The merchants were rich and corpulent, and the women beautiful. When Vesuvius erupted, 20,000 people were stopped in their tracks, and killed on the spot.

You can still see the remains of many people killed almost 2,000 years ago, the expressions on their faces as if they died yesterday. Women cower over their babies, men reach out to protect their wives. Pompeii is a city stuck in time, and with the techniques of modern-day excavation, mostly free to wander and explore. It is much larger than you expect, so bring your walking shoes, and an extra bottle of water. Also, explore the history of Pompeii before you arrive, so you can choose the sites you want to see on your journey. Sights to see include:

The Amphitheater – this hearkens back to the time of gladiators and deadly combat. It is wonderfully preserved.

The House of the Vetti – you want to visit this site for the plethora of multi-colored frescoes. They each tell a story, and you won't want to miss the fresco of the God of Fertility.

The Temple of Apollo – this is a site in Pompeii where you can see artifacts dating from even before the Romans took over, back to the Etruscan time.

Take a look at the website (click on the British flag for the English version) for directions, times, and rates. http://www.pompeiturismo.it/index.php?Itemid=28&id=14&option=com_content&task=view&lang=en

Capri Island

Take a short boat trip out to the island of Capri, and it will be no surprise to you why many celebrities (including Mariah Carey) like to call this little island their home away from home. Capri is in the Gulf of Naples, on the south side, and has been a resort for over 2,000 years. One step on this island and you'll know why people have been coming here for more than two millennia, and why even Napoleon tried to take over the island. You would want to, too.

There are two main cities on Capri. The cities are Capri (with more than 7,000 inhabitants), and Anacapri (about 6,000 inhabitants). If those aren't numbers enough for you, then how about this: 2 million. That's the amount of people who visit Capri each year. It is only 25 minutes from Sorrento, and 50 minutes from Naples by boat, so it's no wonder so many people flock to this gorgeous island on a romantic and beautiful getaway each year.

There are so many things to see and do during your trip to Capri, you may want to stay the night. But a good place to start is with a boat tour around the island, to get a sense of its tiny size, and also a close-up glimpse of the crystal clear waters around the island. A few things you will see include La Grotta Azzurra (the blue grotto), possibly one of the most famous grottoes in the world. If you're lucky, the tide will be low and your boat captain will be courageous, and he will slip your boat underneath the cliff to take a look at the grotto, and its glowing blue water, from inside the island. It is a sight not to be forgotten. You might also see the Natural Arch, which is a beautiful natural formation of rock along the side of the island, and you can be reminded of the natural power of the water.

No trip to Capri is complete without a trip to the "Piazzetta", which translates to "the little piazza." There are cafés, restaurants, newsagents, and a tourism office so that you can buy a newspaper or a guide, a coffee or glass of wine, and kick up your heels and join the town in watching the rest of the world go by. It is a gorgeous place to look at the sunset from a little spot behind the town's ex-cathedral, and you might find that you wish sunset were just a little longer, so that you could just take one more picture, have one more glass of wine. But don't fret. After sunset, the town heats up and you'll have more than enough chances to eat and dance your way to nirvana.

Just moments away from the Piazzetta, you might want to pop into Al Grottino on Via Longano, 27 for a meal that you will not forget. Tuck your head underneath the beautiful white archways and vaulted ceilings to tuck yourself into a dinner that is as marvelous to eat as it is to savor. Expect light traditional Mediterranean fare, local wines, and more specialties than is possible to count. Call them at 081 8370584 to see about reservations.

You can find more about the island of Capri at the website: http://www.capri.com/

Naples

About two hours from Sorrento, you will find a day trip unlike any other to Napoli (Naples). Unlike other places in Italy, even the locals will tell you to hold on to your purses here! Naples is a dark, gritty place, with layer upon layer of history, in some places garbage, buildings, and crypts forming the winding streets and hills of Naples. It is a place unlike any other, and is absolutely massive. It's a good idea that before you come here, you plan your day(s) well, as there is much to do, and you may want to book private transportation, as the public transportation sometimes even smells like it hasn't been cleaned in a few centuries.

One of the things you should do on your trip to Naples is the Castel Nuovo. This is a huge castle built in the 13th century that gives you a true glimpse of what life must have been like those hundreds of years ago. Inside are frescoes and paintings, and more historical artifacts than you're going to know what to do with. For a history buff, this is one sight not to miss.

Address: Via Vittorio Emanuele III 80133 Naples, Italy
Telephone: 081 7955877
http://www.comune.napoli.it/flex/cm/pages/ServeBLOB.php/L/EN/IDPagina/1372

Take the Funiculare, or inclined train, up the hill to the Vomero district. This is a district that is very popular in the evening, and is teeming with locals out for an after-dinner stroll and tourists. You will absolutely want to try a Zeppoli, which is fried bread filled with tomato sauce. This will be a perfect way to stave off dinner for just one more stroll, just one more store.

You will want to visit the Duomo in Naples, which was built in the 1200s and is an excellent example of Gothic architecture. It was built and dedicated to Naples' patron saint, San Gennaro, and directly next to it is the 4th century Basilica, which has amazing frescoes and columns.

Address: Via Duomo, Naples, Province of Naples, Italy
Telephone: 081 449097
http://www.duomodinapoli.it/

Recommendations for the Budget Traveller

Places to Stay

There are quite a few places to stay in the region around Sorrento. Your best bet is to do your research before your visit, and decide how many days you'd like to spend in each location. Here are a few places to get you started.

Sorrento

L'Angolo di Paradiso: One option to consider when you stay in Sorrento is to try a hotel in the Agriturismo movement. This movement aims to place visitors in local homes and farms, for a unique and ecologically sound housing option. L'Angolo di Paradiso, located right smack in the middle of Sorrento, is a beautiful farm surrounded by olives, lemons, and oranges. You can open your window and just feel the mixture of the salt water and lemon trees splash up against your face. There are six bedrooms here, as well as a restaurant that serves local and the freshest of fresh food you could possibly imagine. Breakfast is included, as well, so you can stock up for your busy day of touring.

Address: Via Monticelli, 2 c/o Il Corso Italia 333 - Sorrento 80067
http://www.agriturismo.it/en/farmhouse/campania/naples/LAngolodiParadiso-6190811/contact.html

Another good option, but if you want a "standard" hotel room, with no farm in sight, is the Hotel Il Nido, which has decent prices and has a beautiful view of the sea.

Address: Via Nastro Verde, 62 80067 Sorrento, Province of Naples, Italy
Telephone: 081 8782766
http://www.ilnido.it/

Ravello (Amalfi Coast)

Bed and Breakfast I Limoni: This Bed and Breakfast is in Ravello, which is a good place to stay on your tour of the Amalfi Coast. This is up a hill some ways, but is a great budget choice, and is actually part of a farm that produces lemons. Want to bet they make some great limoncello there? Also included is breakfast.

Address: Via Gradoni 14, San Cosma, Ravello
Telephone: 089 858056
www.bb-ilimoni.com

Pompeii

Hotel Apollo Pompeii is a nice, budget hotel located very close to the ruins of the city, so at the end of a long day of dusty walking, you can kick back and relax in your room, or in one of the hotels restaurants.

Address: Via Carlo Alberto 18, Pompeii
Telephone: 081 863 0309
http://www.hotelapollopompei.com/

Naples

Bed and Breakfast Bonapace Porta Nolana:

This is close to the central station of Naples, so you can arrive then directly afterwards kick off your shoes and unpack. This is a clean, cheap option for those of you wanting to stay in the center of city, which has easy access to the port for trips to Capri, or up the hill to the shopping and restaurants in the Vomero District.

Address: Via San Cosmo Fuori Porta Nolana 4 - Naples
Telephone: 877-662-6988
http://www.bonapaceaccomodation.com/

Places to Eat

It is difficult to choose just a few recommendations for where to eat in the Sorrento area. If you're lucky, your guide along the coast of Amalfi will lead you to a restaurant tucked away in the hills, or on a secluded beach somewhere. Here are some tried and true choices for your time in beautiful Sorrento.

Sant'anna da Emilia

Sant'anna da Emilia is a charming place to get a delicious local meal. It is modestly priced, and is actually located in a former boat shed, adding to its historical appeal. Don't expect any pricey or sophisticated meals here; this trattoria is focused on serving fresh, local foods such as spaghetti with mussels or gnocchi, Sorrento-style. Pair your meal with the house wine, red or white, and sit back and enjoy. Reservations are usually not possible, so arrive before you want to eat if you come in tourist season, or be prepared to wait.

Address: Via Marina Grande 62, Sorrento
Telephone: 081 807 2720

Zi'Antonio

Zi'Antonio, which translates to "Uncle Tony" is a great option for those of you wanting to eat in the fishing village of Sorrento. It is small, and quaint, and its tiny size allows for personalized service at modest process. What makes this restaurant special is its private taxi service, which will send a car to your hotel and drive you back again (just make sure to tip the driver). Expect well-cooked local dishes and a long, lazy meal.

Address: Via Luigi De Maio, 11 – 80067, Sorrento
Telephone: 081 8781623
http://www.zintonio.it/

Taverna Azzura

For a lovely place to eat after bathing to your heart's content in Marina Grande, try Taverna Azzura. It's known for its fried squid, a local favorite, and is located right on the water's edge. It is an extremely short walk from Piazza Tasso, and you will find it small but popular, so arrive ready to wait, or sit on the beach with a bottle of beer and await the local delicacies that will be sampling at dinner. A good idea, if you like seafood, is to try the catch of the day, which will always be prepared very lightly; sautéed with butter and garlic, and perhaps some lemon.

Address: 166 Marina Grande, Sorrento
Telephone: 081 877 2510
Website: www.taverna_azzurra.it

Gelateria Davide

No trip to Italy is complete without at least one gelato (ice cream.) One of the best places to sample some gelato on your journey is the Gelateria Davide. He's been in business since 1957, and you'll find this an ideal place to relax after a long day's touring. Try a coffee while you're there, or a sandwich or cake if you're hungry for more than ice cream.

Address: Sorrento Via P.R. Giuliani, 41 - Sorrento
Telephone: 081 8781337
http://www.davideilgelato.com/

Places to Shop

Tourists have been coming to shop on the Amalfi coast for centuries. From pottery to jewelry, to fabrics and fresh produce and fish, there is no shortage of things to open your purse strings for in Sorrento. So if you're a bit sunburnt and tired of the beach, head back into town and check out the following places:

Macramé

Macramé is located a few steps away from the historic Piazza Tazzo, and is a perfect place to look for lady's fashion, including hats, coats, bags, scarves, and gloves. This store has been open for quite some time, so it is fun to think of what famous people have shopped here before you.

Address: Via Luigi De Maio, 28 80067 Sorrento
Telephone: 081 8773114
http://www.sorrentotour.it/macrame/

Limonoro

It would be a sin to come all the way to Sorrento and at least not sample the local liquor, Limoncello. It probably would be just as bad not to come home with some for your friends and family. Head to Limonoro to find all sorts of lemon liquors and sweets, and other local delicacies to either bring back for your loved ones or keep just for yourself.

Address: Via San Cesareo, 49/53 0067 Sorrento
Telephone: 081 8785348
www.limonoro.it

De Cenzo

If you want to go home with some of Sorrento's beautiful ceramics, then look no further than De Cenzo, which specializes in handicrafts such as ceramics and paintings. Even if you don't go home with anything, it is a special treat to walk through the aisles of this store, gazing at crafts that are just as gorgeous as the treasures you could find in a museum.

Address: Via Tasso, 23 80067 Sorrento
Telephone: 081 8784757
www.decenzo.it

Pompeii

On August 24, 79 AD, the city of Pompeii located near Naples was destroyed by a massive volcanic eruption of Mount Vesuvius. 16,000 people were killed. Lava and ash blanketed the city but preserved its buildings which can be seen by visitors today. Pompeii offers a unique glimpse into the past and is like nowhere else on earth.

For nearly seventeen hundred years, the city lay undisturbed, frozen in time, preserved just as the city was when the volcano erupted.

Every year, Pompeii attracts over two million visitors. Tourists can visit the Amphitheatre, the Temple of Apollo, the Garden of Fugitives together with well-preserved ruins of other ancient buildings.

You could spend several days exploring the ancient city. It is also quite possible to do an adequate tour of Pompeii on a single day trip from nearby Naples or the Amalfi Coast.

Modern day Pompeii also offers other attractions in addition to the ancient ruins. The Sanctuary of the Madonna of the Rosary is a popular tourist attraction and many visitors choose to take in the natural beauty and spend time exploring the mountainside of nearby Mount Vesuvius.

Culture

The city of Pompeii was constructed in the 7th century BC, and was dedicated to Venus, the Roman goddess of sexuality and fertility. The citizens of this city were not shy about their sexuality and brothels were popular in Pompeii, and many Roman and local gentlemen were known to visit them. One brothel still stands among the ruins to this day. This pagan religion is still evident today in the many temples dedicated to different Roman, Greek, and Egyptian gods and goddesses.

Two thousand years ago, wealthy Romans vacationed in Pompeii to enjoy the beautiful weather of the Mediterranean climate.

The city was a thriving center of economy, art, and society and had a population of well over twenty thousand people. Many seemingly modern day amenities were evident in the ancient city, such as restaurants, food markets, and hotels. Many tourists are astounded at the level of sophistication in a city that died out almost two thousand years ago.

Modern day Pompeii was founded in 1891 and currently has a population around twenty-five thousand people. Today, the majority of the population of the population is Catholic. Local people speak Italian with a localized dialect. Since Pompeii is a large tourist town, most of the population also speaks some English. It is not uncommon for members of extended families to live in one household, as the Italian culture stresses the importance of family.

With the still-dangerous volcano looming in the distance, the soil is incredibly fertile and can support a multitude of different crops. This is just on the reasons why over two million people live in the shadow of this massive volcano, knowing full well the dangers they face when a powerful eruption occurs again.

Location & Orientation

Pompeii is located on the coast of the Bay of Naples in Italy. It is a two and a half hour drive southeast from Rome. The city of Naples, with a population of around 900,000, is near to Pompeii in the north. To get to the ruins, most people choose the train. If you are staying in the Pompeii area and wish to go into Naples, one of the three train companies can offer you an inexpensive trip into the city and a round-trip train ticket only costs about $5 USD. There are also taxis and private car rental agencies available. If you decide to use a car, parking lots near the ruins are inexpensive or free. Pompeii is a city that shows a perfect integration of ancient and modern Italy.

Climate & When to Visit

Spring in Pompeii is beautiful. The high temperatures during this season stay between 15°C and 21°C (60°F and 70°F). Pompeii has very little rainfall in the later spring months. This is the best time to visit Pompeii, especially if you plan to spend a large amount of your trip outside.

Summer is much warmer and is a dry season. The high temperatures range from 26°C to 32°C (80°F to 90°F). If you decide to go to Pompeii during the summer, bring sunglasses and sunscreen! This is also a very popular time for tourists, so expect Pompeii to be very crowded during this time. Some weekends of during the summer, crowds as large as 20,000 flock to Pompeii, with an average of 4,000 people coming in on a regular weekend.

If you are not a fan of crowds (or heat), this is not the best time to visit Pompeii.

Fall (Autumn) in Pompeii is the rainy season, so if you decide to travel during this time, bring your umbrella. Temperatures stay above 26°C (80°F) until late October, but usually hover around 21°C or 22°C (70°F-75°F) through the end of November. Travelling in the later fall will help save you money since it is during the off-season for tourism but will still offer most of the attractions of the peak season.

Winter is Pompeii is quite pleasant as far as winters go. Temperatures stay in the upper 50s throughout the winter and the city remains rather dry. If you don't mind the milder weather, winter is a perfect time to visit Pompeii. There will be very few other tourists during the winter and travelling in the off-season is a great way to save money.

Sightseeing Highlights

Ancient Ruins of Pompeii

General Admission Rates to Pompeii:
Adults (24+): €11 (About $14 USD)
School teachers and adults 18-24: €5,50 (About $7 USD
Seniors & Children: Free

Tour Guide Fees:
At the train station: €12 (About $15 USD)
At the gates: €10 (About $13 USD)

If you are not interested in being shown around Pompeii, there are audio tour guides available for rent, as well as tour guidebooks. If you are interested in any of these, merchants will have them available for purchase, and the employees at the gate will have the audio tour guides and books to rent.

Summer Hours: 8:30 am - 7:30 pm
Winter Hours: 8:30 am - 5:00 pm
Closed: January 1st, May 1st, December 25th

Walking is the most common as well as practical way to get around the ruins of Pompeii, but there are a few bicycles available for rent at the front gates. However, bicycles are rather impractical to use in the ancient city since the roads are quite uneven and bumpy.

If you want to take in all of the following sites, you will be walking for the majority of the day. If you are planning on spending the entire day exploring the ruins, make sure wear comfortable shoes and bring plenty of water, especially if visiting during the summer months. The heat can get very uncomfortable, especially when there are no clouds and very few trees to offer protection from the sun.

The following sites are put into the order they appear as you enter in the main gates of the ruins of Pompeii. Many of the following sites have suffered more damage due to earthquakes than the damage caused by the volcano or by time.

Temple of Apollo

As the name suggests, this temple was dedicated to the Greek god of the sun and light. This was the most important place of worship in the ancient city for well over one hundred years. This temple was built in the 3rd century BC and features statues of other gods as well as Apollo.

Temple of Jupiter

This temple was built sometime in the 2nd century BC. This temple overtook the Temple of Apollo as the most important temple in the city around the time of the Roman conquest, in which the entire town became completely Romanised. The basement of this temple held the town's treasury and also had a space dedicated to sacrificial ceremonies. From looking at the remaining architecture of the building, it is easy to imagine how elegant the building was when it was first constructed over two thousand years ago.

Temple of Isis

This temple was not dedicated to a Roman or a Greek god, instead to the Egyptian goddess of magic and nature, Isis. It is believed that women and slaves were the primary worshipers of Isis. This temple was one of the first ruins to be discovered in the 18th century when the ruins were first unearthed. Some of the original sculptures from the building have been moved to the Archeological Museum in Naples.

Street of Tombs

This street was not inside the city walls, as it was forbidden to bury the dead inside of the city in the ancient Roman culture. This stretch has well over thirty tombs and was a site for trade and a main passage for travellers entering or exiting the building. The tombs on this road were decorated in a way that reflected a person's economic status. Families would also go visit the tombs on a regular visit and leave food on the tomb, as a way of sharing their meal with their deceased loved ones.

Stabian Baths

The Stabian Baths dated as far back as the fifth century BCE, long before Pompeii was influenced by Roman culture. Out of the three main baths in Pompeii, this bath was by far the largest and the most grand. It had separate areas for both men and women to exercise, swim, and take heated baths. The baths were in surprisingly good condition at the time of excavation in the eighteenth century, and many artifacts and pieces of art were salvaged from the ruins. For many tourists, this is a very interesting peek at the way the ancient inhabitants lived.

House of Menander

Historians are unsure of who would have owned this house, but if the artwork is any indication, a very wealthy local or visiting Roman most likely owned the house. The paintings on the walls are very intricate and well preserved.

House of Lovers

The House of Lovers is one of the more recently discovered ruins and has been excavated since 1987. This building contains many smaller buildings and worship centers for minor gods and goddesses. There was a bakery as well as a stable in this area. During the excavation, the ovens from the bakery and donkey skeletons were uncovered and remain in their original graves to this day.

Lupanare (Ancient Brothel)

The Lupanare was the biggest of Pompeii's brothels (there were probably nine more). This building is recognized as a brothel with the erotic scenes depicted on the walls and the large amount of graffiti of a sexual nature carved into the walls.

Garden of Fugitives

The Garden of Fugitives is arguably the most moving part of Pompeii. When this part of the ancient city was excavated in 1961, there were thirteen hollow areas in the ash and dirt that perfectly preserved the people in the garden when the volcano hit. Scientists believe that the thirteen people were killed by the toxic gases that the volcano emitted. After the hollow areas were found, they were filled with plaster to forever preserve the positions the deceased were in when they died. These haunting plaster sculptures show the suffering of the people of Pompeii in their final moments of life.

Despite the name suggesting that these people were possibly criminals, these unfortunate individuals included children and the positions they are in suggest they were attempting to shield themselves from the volcanic ash and gas and were unable to get out of the orchard in time. Today, the plaster casts are protected from the elements and the tourists inside a small building.

Mount Vesuvius

Mount Vesuvius was the volcano that made Pompeii and it's neighboring cities infamous in the first century. Today, it remains the sole active volcano on the mainland of Europe. This volcano has erupted about fifty times throughout its lifetime. A little over 100 years ago, Mount Vesuvius experienced it's most recent major eruption, in which it killed over two thousand people.

Mount Vesuvius soars 1277 m (4190 ft) into the air. For those who enjoy hiking, it is a climb that is manageable in under an hour of strenuous walking. When you get to the top of the volcano, however, you won't want to come back down. The view from the top of the mountain is simply breathtaking. For those who do not want to or are unable to climb to the top of the mountain, there are many agencies in the area or out of Naples that offer bus rides up to the top of the basin so that everyone can have the chance to see its massive crater.

Mount Vesuvius is one of the most recommended sites by past tourists to the area.

Sanctuary of Madonna of the Rosary

Piazza Bartolo Longo, 1
80045 Pompeii (NA)
Tel. (+39) 081 8577111
E-mail: info@santuariodipompei.it

No admission fee to tour this site.

This beautiful sanctuary was finished in 1901 after nearly thirty years of construction on the massive dome. Reported miracles have occurred at this shrine and have been attributed to the Blessed Virgin Mary. It is an important site for many Catholics from around the world. Even if you aren't Catholic, you are invited to take a look around the famous cathedral. However, the cathedral staff request that photographs are not taken inside of the church. The cathedral is rather unassuming from the outside but on the inside, there are magnificent works of art painted onto the walls and ceiling. This space can comfortably seat six thousand individuals, but still cannot always accommodate all who want to worship here on holidays and during festivals.

Naples Day Trip

Naples is the largest city in Southern Italy. It has a central location convenient to other popular towns and interesting places for tourists such as the Bay of Naples and Pompeii. This makes it a perfect location for vacationers to use as home base while in the Amalfi Coast region. In addition, it has numerous major train lines, a bus station, and flights going to various destinations in Italy. It holds many historical and artistic treasures and an abundance of museums, architecture, castles, shopping and churches.

Naples is known to have some of the finest theater and opera houses in the world. The oldest and most beautiful one that is still operating is Teatro di San Carlo. It was built in 1816 and after burning down it was rebuilt in 1845. It is now restored to its amazing original beauty with an unbelievable gold and red interior. Because of an abundance of outdoor monuments and historic statues, Naples is sometimes referred to as an open-air museum.

Spaccanapoli is a neighborhood in Naples that features streets and alleys crowded with colorful shops. You will find anything from colorful clothing, rosaries, and artisan workshops, to delicious seafood. It is also famous for its nativity scenes.

Piazza del Plebiscito

This 19th century plaza is one of the biggest and well-known tourist sites in Naples, as well as an area of authentic Italian culture. This plaza was built in the early nineteenth century.

On the eastern side of the plaza lies the Royal Palace and statues of famous ancient kings of Naples line the outside edges of the plaza. To the western side lies the massive church of San Francesco di Paola, and is a testament to the very Catholic country. Both of these buildings are considered incredibly important pieces of architecture and history for Naples.

Museo Archeologico Nazionale

Piazza Museo, 19,
80135 Naples, Italy
Telephone: (+39) 081 4422149

Hours: Wednesday- Monday: 9:00 am - 7:00 pm
Tuesday: Closed
Closed January 1st, May 1st, and December 25th

General Admission Rates:
Adults: €6.5 (About $8.50)
Seniors and Students are eligible for discounted admissions

The National Museum of Archeology is an incredibly famous site in Naples. This museum holds some of the oldest and most valuable statues, works of art, and artifacts. Many of the more fragile pieces from Pompeii that cannot be exposed to the elements have been moved to this museum, such as artwork from the Temple of Isis or paintings from walls of buildings. It also holds a realistic model of what Pompeii would have looked like before the eruption. This museum is the perfect way to start or end your learning journey.

Of course, there is more to the archeology of Italy than just the ruins of Pompeii. There are artifacts dating as far back as the Paleolithic period. The Paleolithic period was the time in history where historians and archeologists can definitively say that human started using primitive tools to aid in everyday life.

Amalfi

The town of Amalfi is located about 29 miles from Naples. The Festival of Saint Andrew (25-27 June, and 30 November) is held in Amalfi. The Crypt of St. Andrew is contained in the Cathedral of Amalfi. The church's crypt is reputed to hold parts of St. Andrew's body who was a disciple of Jesus.

Also in Amalfi is MuseodellaCarta, which is housed in a 13th-century paper mill (the oldest in Europe). The original paper presses are preserved and are still in full working order. Visitors are able to witness the entire papermaking process. The paper can be purchased in the gift shop.

The Byzantine New Year's celebration is in the town of Amalfi (31 August). The annual celebration makes the village come alive. Included are medieval plays, duels between fighters with sticks, water races, and rope pulls. Musical and theatrical performances are also enjoyed on this two-day celebration.

Positano

Positano is located on one of the most stunning areas of the Amalfi Coast. It is a small picturesque town built on the cliffs and winding down to the coast. Due to the cliffside location, Positano offers some of the most unforgettable views on Amalfi Coast. While you are there, the views will seem almost unreal. Therefore, gazing at these views will be one of your favorite things to do.

Adding to that beauty are the brightly painted houses that cling to the cliffs and are reflected in the clear water of the sea. There are thousands of steps cut into the cliffs. They can be taken down to the water or other parts of the town. Some of those steps are as steep as a ladder.

Another reason travelers come to Positano is to shop at the numerous women's clothing shops. The sea of colorful, authentic, and handmade clothing is quite an impressive site for a shopper.

The church of Santa Maria Assunta is a must see. It features a splendid bell tower and a majestic dome with tiles of green and yellow. The church was built in the 10th century and redone in the 18th century. This is only one of many magnificent churches in the area.

Other churches include the Church of St Matthew covered in stucco and featuring red pilasters. In addition is the Church of St. James, which dates back to the 12th century. Located on the road to Fornillo Beach is the small Church of Santa Margherita with a floor of floral images in terracotta tiles. That is just naming a few. It could take an entire day just to see the churches in Positano.

Ravello

Between June and mid-September, the Ravello Festival, also known as the Wagner Festival, turns much of the town into a performance stage. The Wagner name was derived because of the visit of the German composer Richard Wagner in 1880. The visit was to promote tourism in the area to help the economy. The annual festival began in 1953. Festivities include orchestral concerts, ballet performances, film screenings, and exhibitions.

Also located in Ravello's is the Ravello Cathedral built in 1086. Once inside, the floor sharply inclines in order to give a better view of the amazing architecture and ornate design. On the exterior is featured two bronze doors created in the year 1179.The doors are engraved with the 54 scenes of Christ's life. There are only 24 of these doors in Italy.

An addition, an interesting sight to see in Ravello is the Villa Ravello. It was built by the Ravello family in the 11th century and has been added to for many generations. It now contains art exhibits and the grounds have flowering gardens, which is a gorgeous backdrop for outdoor concerts.

Something different and fun that many people do in Ravello is to take a cooking class. One of the most popular is Mamma Agata's Cooking Class. The first thing you will do is to drink coffee and eat the best lemon cake ever.

You will then move into the kitchen to help prepare a most amazing meal. In addition, you will learn many Italian cooking tricks. The meal consists of appetizers and numerous courses. Most of your time will be spent watching and learning, but the best part is the tasting and drinking.

The conclusion will be to feast on the resulting meal, fit for a queen, along with lemoncello and wine.

Solerno

Solerno became famous for being the location of the world's first medical university. Salerno is also known as an important center for art, culture, and learning, dating back to the 16th century. The churches of Solerno are one of the main attractions including the Salerno Cathedral, which is the most visited church with its large bell tower in the city's center.

San Gregorio Church is a 10th century structure, which holds the Museum of the Medical School of Salerno. Chiesadella SS. Annuziata was built in the 14th century and is situated near the entrance to the old city. This church's main feature is also a beautiful bell tower designed by Ferdinando San Felice.

Blue Grotto, Capri

Definitely not to be missed, the Blue Grotto is called "La Grotta Azzurra" by the locals. It is located on the shores of Anacapri.

The Grotto is a cave that measures approximately 75 feet wide and 180 feet long. The only way to access this cave is by boat.

It is possible to take a tour to the Grotto, but the conditions have to be just right in order to enter the cave. A boat will barely fit through the entrance of the cave. Therefore, you will be required to lay flat on the bottom of the boat when going through the entrance.

The swell of the waves can also make getting through a bit tricky. The gondolier has to wait and go between two waves when the water is lowest. He then pulls the boat through with ropes attached to the wall.

In addition, the weather conditions have to be clear and sunny, or the cave will be enclosed in darkness. If you are lucky enough to find all those requirements happening at the same time, you will be rewarded with an unforgettable experience. Once inside, there is a blue or green light shining in on the clear water and illuminating the stalagmites and stalactites.

Recommendations for the Budget Traveller

Places To Stay

Hotel Diana Pompeii

Vicolo Sant'Abbondio 12, 80045 Pompeii, Italy

This is a perfect place to stay while in Pompeii. A room with a single bed will cost between €40 and €80 ($50 USD to $100 USD). Rooms include television, mini fridge, and mini-bar.

The hotel also offers breakfasts and Wi-Fi internet connection. Another reason this spot is so highly recommended by travel agencies and past travelers is because it is only a five to ten minute walk to the ruins from Hotel Diana Pompeii. This can count down immensely on transportation expenses while you are staying in Pompeii.

Hotel Forum

Via Roma 99,
Pompeii 80045 Italia
Telephone: (+39) 0818501170
Email: info@hotelforum.it

Hotel Forum is another hotel that is located in Pompeii that is just a short walk away from both the ruins of ancient Pompeii and the Sanctuary of the Madonna of the Rosary. Being so close to touristy sites also means you are close to amazing food vendors and great places to shop for souvenirs.

Hotel Forum is a little more expensive, and runs about €100 ($130 USD) per night. However, this hotel does offer a fifteen percent discount if you book your room more than a month in advance of your arrival to Pompeii.

Hotel Palma

Via Piave 15,
80045 Pompeii Italy
Telephone: (+39) 081 8631168
email: info@pompeihotelpalma.com

Hotel Palma was built in the late nineteenth century. Like the other hotels in the area, it is located very close to the ruins as well as the Cathedral. An added perk of this hotel is that the hotel offers free parking to it's guests, so you will not have to pay to keep your car there overnight or when you are visiting the ruins, which is a hidden surprise for many tourists in Pompeii.

A single bedroom costs about €95 per night ($125 USD). There are also discounts available when you book well ahead of time. The hotel features a breakfast buffet, a restaurant, and a bar.

Albergo Pace Pompeii Hotel

Via Sacra 29,
80045 Pompeii, Italy
Telephone: (+39) 081 8636025
Email: info@albergopacepompei.it

With rooms starting at €35 per night ($45 USD), this is the cheapest hotel on this list. The hotel comes with all of the necessities, plus free Wi-Fi connection. Not only will this hotel provide you with a wonderful stay, but they also offer useful maps of the city. Again, this hotel is not far from the Pompeii ruins and from the Cathedral.

Hotel Astoria

Viale Giuseppe Mazzini 87,
80045 Pompeii, Italy
Telephone: (+39) 081 8631074
Email: info@hotelastoriapompei.it

Hotel Astoria is another affordable hotel, conveniently located downtown. They have a restaurant, bar, and room service available, along with free Wi-Fi connection in the whole hotel.

This hotel offers a close location to the tourist attractions, free parking, and a complimentary shuttle to and from the airport should you require one. Single rooms start at about €40 per night (about $55 USD). If you are traveling with your family, this hotel is accommodating for those who need space.

Places To Eat

Ristorante Pizzeria Carlo Alberto

Via Carlo Alberto 15,
80045 Pompeii, Italy
Telephone: (+39) 081 8633231

If you are looking for a place to get great pizza, this is the place. These pizzas are inexpensive, all under €7.5 ($10 USD) and will feed two people. There are also many other fantastic and inexpensive entrees on the menu, with the most expensive meat dish running about €15 ($20 USD) and most significantly less. A fantastic choice if you are also looking for a great dessert or a glass of Italian wine.

Ristorante Al Gamberone

Via Piave, 36
80045 Pompeii Italy
Telephone: (+39) 081 8506814

If you are looking for inexpensive, authentic Italian food, Al Gamberone is the place to go. Owned by locals who appreciate simple pasta and meat dishes, few are dissatisfied with the quality of their food or the service.

Roadside Stands

Outside of the main gates of Pompeii, there are many food vendors who set up stands to entice hungry and thirsty tourists. For the most part the food is authentic and good, and not overpriced.

You cannot beat this when you are in a hurry perhaps before visiting the ruins. There are plenty of local Italians who eat at these roadside stands, which speaks to the authenticity of the food served.

Printed in Great Britain
by Amazon